I0815759

DISCOVERING THE UNITED STATES

Kansas

BY GEORGE ANTHONY KULZ

An Imprint of Abdo Publishing
abdobooks.com

abdobooks.com

Printed in China.
052024
092024

Cover Photo: Sean Pavone/Shutterstock Images
Interior Photos: kansasmemory.org/Kansas State Historical Society, 4–5; Shutterstock Images, 7, 26; Brian Lasenby/Shutterstock Images, 8 (top left); Ann Cantelow/Shutterstock Images, 8 (top right); Sari ONeal/Shutterstock Images, 8 (bottom left); O. S. Fisher/Shutterstock Images, 8 (bottom right); Francis Lavigne-Theriault/iStockphoto, 10; Mark Reinstein/Alamy, 12–13; Sarin Images/Granger Historical Picture Archive, 14; Brent Hofacker/Shutterstock Images, 16; Master Sgt. John Gordinier/US Air Force/DVIDS, 18; Rodney Todt/Alamy, 20–21; Wasan Ritthawon/Shutterstock Images, 22; Brian Lawdermilk/Getty Images Sport/Getty Images, 24; Sue Smith/Shutterstock Images, 28 (top left); Red Line Editorial, 28 (top right), 29 (top); Sean Pavone/Shutterstock Images, 28 (bottom); Real Window Creative/Shutterstock Images, 29 (bottom)

Editor: Marley Richmond
Series Designer: Katharine Hale

Library of Congress Control Number: 2023949346

Publisher's Cataloging-in-Publication Data

Names: Kulz, George Anthony, author.
Title: Kansas / by George Anthony Kulz
Description: Minneapolis, Minnesota: Abdo Publishing, 2025 | Series: Discovering the United States | Includes online resources and index.
Identifiers: ISBN 9781098293864 (lib. bdg.) | ISBN 9798384913139 (ebook)
Subjects: LCSH: U.S. states--Juvenile literature. | Kansas--History--Juvenile literature. | Midwest States—Juvenile literature. | Physical geography--United States--Juvenile literature.
Classification: DDC 973--dc23

All population data taken from:
"Estimates of Population by Sex, Race, and Hispanic Origin: April 1, 2020 to July 1, 2022." *US Census Bureau, Population Division,* June 2023, census.gov.

CONTENTS

CHAPTER 1
Welcome to Kansas 4

CHAPTER 2
The People of Kansas 12

CHAPTER 3
Places in Kansas 20

State Map 28
Glossary 30
Online Resources 31
Learn More 31
Index 32
About the Author 32

William Purvis and Charles Wilson stand next to their flying machine in Goodland, Kansas.

Welcome to Kansas

It is Thanksgiving Day in November 1909. Nearly the whole town of Goodland, Kansas, has gathered. William Purvis and Charles Wilson have created a new invention. It is a special vehicle, and they want to show it off.

The vehicle has a flat platform with a pole in the center. There are two **propellers** on the pole. Each propeller has two wings that look like fan blades. Purvis and Wilson start a small engine. To everyone's surprise, the vehicle's propellers begin to turn. The vehicle jumps up and down. It can't fly yet. But it will become one of the world's first helicopters.

Today, the High Plains Museum in Goodland has a **replica** of this helicopter. This is just one of many Kansas attractions.

The Land of Kansas

Kansas is in the Midwest region of the United States. It is landlocked. This means it is almost or entirely surrounded by land. Kansas is bordered

Bison can be seen across Kansas.

by four states. Nebraska lies to the north. Missouri is to the east. Oklahoma is to the south. Colorado is to the west.

Kansas Facts

DATE OF STATEHOOD
January 29, 1861

CAPITAL
Topeka

POPULATION
2,937,150

AREA
82,278 square miles
(213,100 sq km)

STATE BIRD

Western meadowlark

STATE TREE

Cottonwood

STATE FLOWER

Wild native sunflower

STATE ANIMAL

American bison

Each US state has a different population, size, and capital city. States also have state symbols.

Kansas is home to many different landscapes. The state is known for its rolling hills and plains. The western part of the state has dry plains. Some plains are good for farming.

Other areas have rolling hills, cliffs, and mountains. The southeast part of the state is very wet and filled with forests and rocky areas.

Climate of Kansas

Kansas summers are often very warm. The winters are not too cold. Kansas is a windy state. It has the second-largest number of tornadoes in the United States.

The Middle of the United States

The exact middle of the **continental** United States is in Lebanon, Kansas. This point is marked with a monument and a US flag. This landmark is close to the Nebraskan border.

About 90 tornadoes hit Kansas every year. Most tornadoes strike during April, May, and June.

The amount of rain and snow in Kansas depends on the area. The western part of the state is often drier than the east. Kansas gets far less snowfall than what is usual in the United States.

Explore Online

Visit the website below. What new information did you learn about Kansas that wasn't in Chapter One?

Kansas

abdocorelibrary.com/discovering-kansas

The Kanza people held a celebration on their original Kansas homeland in 2015. Many people wore traditional clothing.

The People of Kansas

The first people of Kansas were American Indians. For thousands of years, eight Native peoples lived there. They included the Osage, Pawnee, Wichita, and Kanza (or Kaw). *Kanza* means "people of the south wind." This is where Kansas got its name.

European settlers began setting up towns in Kansas in the 1700s. Wichita was founded in 1864.

European **settlers** arrived in Kansas in the 1700s. They eventually forced most American Indian peoples out of the region. Today, Kansas has four federally recognized tribes. But none are the original peoples from Kansas. They are all recognized in the states they moved to.

People of Kansas Today

In the late 1800s and early 1900s, many Mexicans came to Kansas. Some were moving **cattle** from Texas. Others traveled along the Santa Fe Trail. This trail connected Missouri and New Mexico. It passed through Kansas. Many travelers stopped there.

Today, the state is home to almost 3 million people. Nearly 86 percent of Kansas's population is white. About 13 percent of Kansans are Hispanic or Latino. About 6 percent are Black, and 3 percent are Asian. A little over 1 percent are American Indian or Alaska Native.

Bierocks are traditionally from Russia. They became popular in Germany.

Some famous people are from Kansas. Amelia Earhart was born in Atchison in 1897. She was the first woman to fly solo across the Atlantic Ocean.

Kansas Culture

Many surveys have named Kansas one of the friendliest states. People from Kansas are sometimes called Jayhawkers. A jayhawk is an imaginary mix of a jay and a hawk. Jays and hawks are loud and violent birds. The nickname started in the mid-1800s to describe groups during the American Civil War (1861–1865).

Kansas has many unique foods. Chili served with cinnamon rolls is a popular dish in Kansas. Bierocks are flavorful pocket sandwiches brought over by German settlers in the 1870s. They are filled with beef, cabbage, onions, spices, and cheese.

Fictional People from Kansas

Two famous characters from fiction lived in Kansas. One is the comic book character Superman. The other is Dorothy from the book *The Wizard of Oz*. Like many Kansans, Superman valued kindness. Dorothy's famous movie quote is, "There's no place like home."

The McConnell Air Force Base in Wichita, Kansas, hosts an air show every year. Pilots perform routines with their planes.

Businesses in Kansas

Kansas is one of the largest wheat growers in the United States. It is also one of the largest beef and salt producers. Kansas is known for producing cement and stone for construction as well.

Wichita, Kansas, is called the Air Capital of the World. One-third of US airplanes are made in the state. Kansas ranks third in the number of **aviation** workers in the United States. Kansas's companies also provide training and planes for the US military.

Further Evidence

Look at the website below. Does it give any new evidence to support Chapter Two?

Kaw

abdocorelibrary.com/discovering-kansas

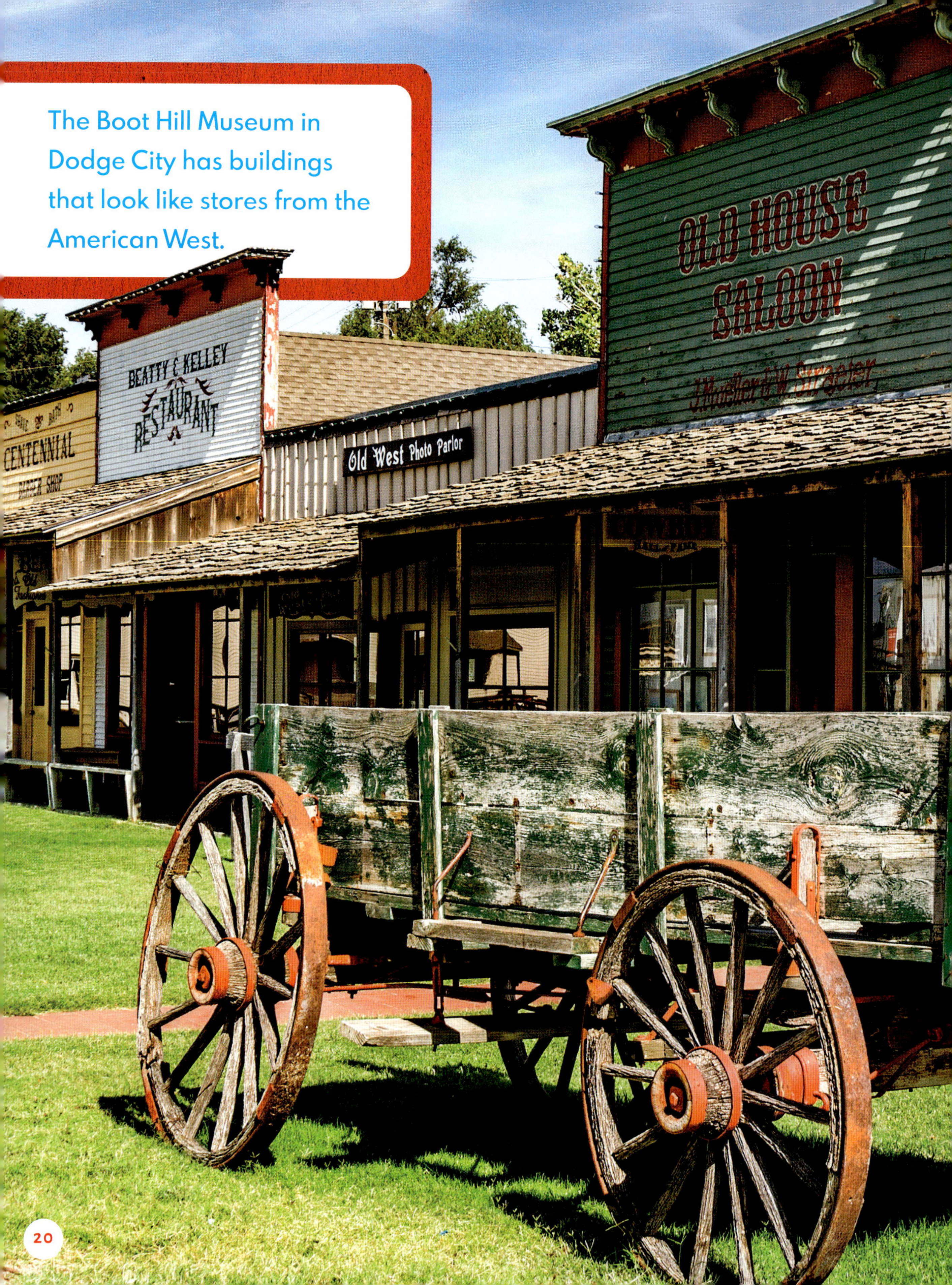

The Boot Hill Museum in Dodge City has buildings that look like stores from the American West.

Places in Kansas

Kansas is home to some interesting attractions. There are many places to learn about the history of the area. One town to visit in southwest Kansas is Dodge City. Visitors today can see what the American West looked like in the late 1800s.

The Kansas state flag shows what life was like shortly after European settlers came to the state.

They can see replicas of old **saloons** where cowboys once spent time.

The Mine Creek Civil War Battlefield is in Pleasanton, Kansas. The museum teaches visitors about one of the largest battles of the American Civil War (1861–1865). The *Brown v. Board of Education* National Historical Site is in Topeka. Here people can learn about the court decision that ended the separation of Black and white students in schools.

The Pawnee Indian Museum is near Republic, Kansas. Visitors can see an earth lodge where Pawnee people once lived. Visitors can also listen to **authentic** Pawnee music.

Popular Places to Visit

There are many other unique places to visit in Kansas. The Kansas City area is split between Missouri and Kansas. There is a town named Kansas City on either side of the border.

Kansas Speedway hosts two NASCAR race weekends each year. The NASCAR Truck Series is a popular event where drivers race in pickup trucks.

On the Kansas side, people can visit the Kansas Speedway. It hosts many NASCAR racing events. Visitors can also travel the KCK Legacy Trail.

It has information about the different people that make up Kansas City.

Wichita, Kansas, is the largest city in Kansas. One of its most famous attractions is the *Keeper of the Plains* sculpture. The statue is 44 feet (13 m) tall. It was built by a Native Wichita artist. Its location is sacred to the Wichita people.

Strange and Unusual Attractions

Kansas has its share of the world's largest things. The state has the world's largest painting on an easel. It has the world's longest yellow brick road, inspired by *The Wizard of Oz*. Kansas even has the world's largest ball of twine. It is more than 40 feet (12 m) around!

Monument Rocks is a National Natural Monument in Kansas.

Kansas is full of history and natural beauty. Visitors can learn about the American Indian peoples who first lived in the area. They can also try popular foods such as bierocks. There is something for everyone in Kansas.

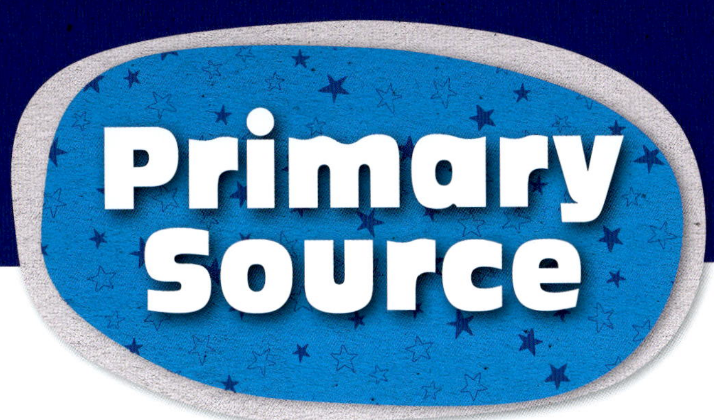

A Kansas tourism website describes reasons why people love the state. It says:

> In addition to the [beautiful] outdoors and charming towns, are the historic sites, landmarks, and museums. . . . Kansas history is a huge part of American history. There's no place like Kansas.

Source: "10 Reasons to Fall in Love with Kansas." *Kansas Tourism*, 31 Jan. 2018, travelks.com. Accessed 18 Oct. 2023.

Point of View

What is the author's point of view on this topic? What is your point of view? Write a short essay about how they are similar and different.

State Map

Lebanon

KEY

Capital
Park
City or town
Point of interest

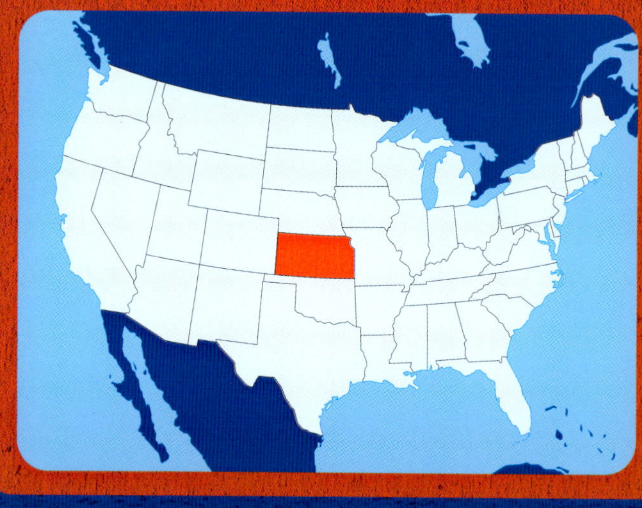

Keeper of the Plains Sculpture

Kansas: The Sunflower State

Nebraska
Missouri
Missouri River
Pawnee Indian Museum
Lebanon
Goodland
Kansas City
Topeka
Colorado
Kansas River
Monument Rocks
Kansas Speedway
Kaw Mission
Mine Creek Civil War Battlefield
Arkansas River
Keeper of the Plains sculpture
Dodge City
Wichita
N
W
E
S
Oklahoma

Topeka

Glossary

authentic
real and original

aviation
related to flying aircraft

cattle
cows and bulls

continental
relating to the lower 48 US states on the North American continent

propeller
a spinning device with blades attached to it

replica
an exact copy of something

saloons
places where people can buy drinks

settlers
people who moved to a new area

Online Resources

To learn more about Kansas, visit our free resource websites below.

Visit **abdocorelibrary.com** or scan this QR code for free Common Core resources for teachers and students, including vetted activities, multimedia, and booklinks, for deeper subject comprehension.

Visit **abdobooklinks.com** or scan this QR code for free additional online weblinks for further learning. These links are routinely monitored and updated to provide the most current information available.

Learn More

Kavon, Kana. *The 50 States.* DK, 2021.

Murray, Julie. *Kansas.* Abdo, 2020.

Weso, Tom Pecore. *Native American Stories for Kids.* Rockridge, 2022.

Index

aviation, 19

bierocks, 17, 26

Dodge City, 21–22

Goodland, 5–6

Kansas City, 23, 25
Kansas Speedway, 24
Kanza people, 13
Keeper of the Plains sculpture, 25

Mine Creek Civil War Battlefield, 22–23

plains, 6, 8
Purvis, William, 5–6

settlers, 14, 17

Topeka, 8, 23
tornadoes, 9

Wichita people, 13, 25
Wilson, Charles, 5–6

About the Author

George Anthony Kulz is a member of the Society of Children's Book Writers and Illustrators. He writes for children and adults. In his free time, he enjoys hiking, traveling, and spending time with his family.